M000024820

Unrelated Individuals Forming a Group Waiting to Cross

PENGUIN BOOKS

UNRELATED INDIVIDUALS FORMING A GROUP
WAITING TO CROSS

Mark Yakich has worked in the European Parliament in
Brussels and has degrees in political science, West Euro-
pean studies, and poetry. He lives in Oakland, California.
His Web site is www.markyakich.com.

THE NATIONAL POETRY SERIES

The National Poetry Series was established in 1978 to ensure the publication of five poetry books annually through participating publishers. Publication is funded by the late James A. Michener, the Copernicus Society of America, Edward J. Piszek, the Lannan Foundation, the National Endowment for the Arts, and the Tiny Tiger Foundation.

2003 Competition Winners

STEPHEN CRAMER of Astoria, New York, *Shiva's Drum*
Chosen by Grace Schulman, to be published by University of Illinois
Press

ANDREW FELD of Eugene, Oregon, *Citizen*
Chosen by Ellen Bryant Voigt, to be published by HarperCollins
Publishers

RAYMOND MCDANIEL of Ann Arbor, Michigan, *Entrance to Murder and After*
Chosen by Anselm Hollo, to be published by Coffee House Press

JOHN SPAULDING of Phoenix, Arizona, *The White Train: Poems from Photographs*
Chosen by Henry Taylor, to be published by Louisiana State University
Press

MARK YAKICH of Oakland, California, *Unrelated Individuals Forming a Group Waiting to Cross*
Chosen by James Galvin, to be published by Penguin Books

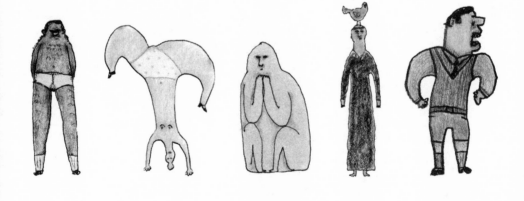

Unrelated Individuals Forming a Group Waiting to Cross

Mark Yakich

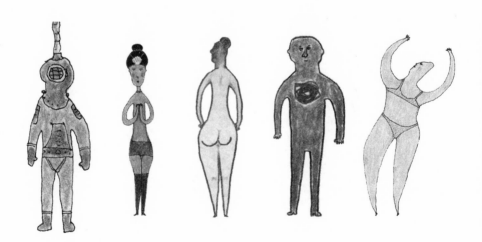

PENGUIN BOOKS

PENGUIN BOOKS

Published by the Penguin Group

Penguin Group (USA) Inc., 375 Hudson Street, New York, New York 10014, U.S.A.

Penguin Books Ltd, 80 Strand, London WC2R 0RL, England

Penguin Books Australia Ltd, 250 Camberwell Road, Camberwell, Victoria 3124, Australia

Penguin Books Canada Ltd, 10 Alcorn Avenue, Toronto, Ontario, Canada M4V 3B2

Penguin Books India (P) Ltd, 11 Community Centre, Panchsheel Park, New Delhi – 110 017, India

Penguin Group (NZ), cnr Airborne and Rosedale Roads, Albany, Auckland 1310, New Zealand

Penguin Books (South Africa) (Pty) Ltd, 24 Sturdee Avenue, Rosebank, Johannesburg 2196, South Africa

Penguin Books Ltd, Registered Offices:
80 Strand, London WC2R 0RL, England

First published in Penguin Books 2004

10 9 8 7 6 5 4 3 2 1

Copyright © Mark Yakich, 2004
All rights reserved

Page 75 constitutes an extension of this copyright page.

LIBRARY OF CONGRESS CATALOGING IN PUBLICATION DATA
Yakich, Mark.
    Unrelated individuals forming a group waiting to cross / Mark Yakich.
        p.   cm.—(National poetry series)
    ISBN 0 14 20.0451 0
        I. Title. II. Series.
    PS3625.A38U57 2004
    811'.6—dc22   2003068914

Printed in the United States of America
Set in Albertina MT
Designed by Sabrina Bowers

Except in the United States of America, this book is sold subject to the condition that it shall not, by way of trade or otherwise, be lent, re-sold, hired out, or otherwise circulated without the publisher's prior consent in any form of binding or cover other than that in which it is published and without a similar condition including this condition being imposed on the subsequent purchaser.

The scanning, uploading, and distribution of this book via the Internet or via any other means without the permission of the publisher is illegal and punishable by law. Please purchase only authorized electronic editions and do not participate in or encourage electronic piracy of copyrighted materials. Your support of the author's rights is appreciated.

For my parents

Contents

III

Ah! They want a light that's better than the sun's!

They want fields that are greener than these!

They want flowers lovelier than these I see!

For me this sun, these fields, and these flowers are enough,

But if they weren't enough,

What I would want is a sun more sun than the sun.

—FERNANDO PESSOA

Unrelated Individuals Forming a Group Waiting to Cross

I

The Mountain

after Balthus

After eating the large bowl
        of potatoes and olives,
                the young girl took
an inordinately long nap
        under a wool blanket.
                Her center was very warm
but the night was beginning
        to get very cold.
                Nothing
unusual there except for
        the moment she turned
                over and half-woke
looking for her brother
        for she had no brother.
                She didn't rise
until early morning,
        just in time to knife-sharpen
                her pencils to fine points
before her art lessons.
        When she stepped
                into the classroom
her peers made fun of
        how she took out
                and set down
her work: A compass
        of her father's
                salmon-lipped kisses.
But the girl did not break.
        She began to draw,
                winter into summer,
handkerchiefs into
        blue lilies, sad men
                into sleeves.

You Are Not a Statue

And I am not a pedestal.

We are not a handful of harmless
scratches on pale pink canvas.
Today is not the day to stop

looking for the woman
to save you. What was once
ivory is wood. What was once

whalebone is cotton.
My coif and corset are duly
fastened, and your shirttail is

tied in a diamond knot.
You may be the giver
of unappreciated nicknames

and the devoted artist
who has given my still life
life. But we can never reach

each other's standards.
You want to condemn me
to eternity. I want to make you

no more perfect than you
used to be. We are not
together, we are not alone.

The Sunset

"Our first and last walk uphill
was for possession of two yellowing plums," she said.

"No, two brown flowers," he said.

"Okay. Two brown flowers.
We climbed slowly toward the house of destiny . . ."

"No, no, the temple of chance . . ." he said.

"All right. Toward the temple of chance.
And in the other direction, two stones rolled downhill," she said.

"Billiard balls. They were billiard balls," he said.

"Oh yes, I recall. It was exactly then,
that I made fun of your sunburn," she said.

"And dropped the plums," he said.

When you made so much of nothing.

The Departure

"Vanishing is what we do best, is us at our best," Brother said
to Sister, who already felt slighted by his temporal touch.

"That's always kept me going," he said, "leavings—what's one more
log on the fire?" Sister, nicknamed the Invisible Man's Daughter,

fetched water in thimbles, trying to close the distance between
them. A bottomless glass and a bathroom with three locking doors.

When Brother was young, when he had not yet invented departure,
they readily made amends. Brother had habitually relied on

his eyes for affection. But now, he exchanged security for
curiosity and wanted his eyes as thin as a book with its pages torn

out and scattered. He proposed a final toast to Sister and him:
"To you, then me—for genealogy is the second most popular hobby

after coin collecting. Something, when young, I was settled with."
Sister said, "When you leave there will be only one of us, and

you'll not be able to love me as easily as tossing pennies down a well."

Postcard to Ricardo and His Daughter Echo

after a painting by Adolphe William Bouguereau

I don't understand why the painter named her
"At the Foot of the Cliff."
I may never understand the French,
but I would have called her
"The Baker's Daughter" on general principle
that she had to get up very early.

There she sits on a block of saltpeter.
Indifferent, she slouches. Hands crossed,
well, fingers really. She must be about six.
And her feet are crossed too, pointed
outward and opposite her head.
And she's bitten her lips licorice red.

She turns to me, *If I have to squat*
on concrete, at least let me be in the city.
So I drop her in the mailbox
hoping she comes out the other end,
looking—oh, how should I say this—
looking at least more ambivalent.

Before Losing Yourself Completely to Love

Drop bread crumbs around your feet.
You will find yourself far away and hungry.

Dreams Hardly Ever Seem to Change Things for the Better

Fantasies, on the other hand, have more to do
with reality than most people like to admit.
A fantasy can take on novel proportions, though
a fantasy and a novel differ in that a fantasy is more

colorful: there are usually more splenetic greens,
hyperbolic blues, and lion yellows than in a novel.
Most novelists deny themselves the color yellow
in particular, whether they are American novelists

abstaining from yellow due to cowardly connotations
or they are Germans for whom yellow is traditionally
the color of courage and thus restrained for history's sake.
Of course, the Egyptians have always loved yellow

but they've only recently produced decent novelists
so it's too early to tell whether any color theory
of yellow holds up across cultures. And yet, yellow
does seem to illuminate everything in this world

when illumination is called for. Take, for instance,
the very marrow of our bones: yellow. Or just look
at the outline of any one thing in the room—
do you not detect a yellow trim, even in the shadows?

Blazon

Save the brightest colors for the smallest bones.
The lightest for the largest.

In general, apply light tones except for on E,
G, and H. Careful on the pubic.

Use pink or red for I
And somber colors for U, V, and X.

Daub the two upper views of the oral cavity
Simultaneously.

The asterisks preceding titles F, J, and L
Refer to footnotes, not to the color blue.

The skull might look larger in winter
Hues, garnet or evergreen.

Color the papillae of the tongue with the same color
Of the tongue (I), but not the tongue itself.

To the right of these notes,
Rub the entire epidermis gray.

The Invisible Man's Daughter

The Invisible Man, it turns out, had a daughter.
She was twelve when I was thirteen

and would come by our house after school on Thursdays.
I thought she was a happy girl until one Thursday

she stood over me in my tree house and said,
"You are more precious to me than my eyes."

Caught without a plan, I walked right in:
"Has your father already disappeared?" I asked.

"Yes," she said, "while bicycling and giving the trees names,
he died. And now the ground I walk on is very dusty."

I moved to hold her hand but could feel nothing.
Little did I know, this was the plan.

Prose Sonnet

He will engineer the sunrise, take apart the clouds as if unbuttoning his shirt. On the way to your house, he will bend down, tie his shoes like framing a picture. He will clip flowers, with his teeth, from the neighbor's garden. He will discard them before reaching your house. He will descend the hill pretending not to be watched as you watch him from the smallest attic window.

But you will not see him round the final curve. Before letting him in, you will forget to ask him to replace the pebbles he's kept in his hip pocket with the heavy rock near the mailbox. Because you are already in love, "Sit down," you will say, pointing to the chair, "no, don't kiss me, it won't be necessary."

The Ordinary Sun

Outdoors, a couple copulated
        openly. Not old, but not
                newly in love either.
Those who were watching
        closed their eyes; those
                who were in a hurry
stopped. And absence,
        which was hiding
                like a boy after stealing
his father's razor,
        to an unknown end,
                made light work hard.

Blind Girl's Litany

I am a pale black figure fondling the smallest mountaintops of
the world.

Yes. A voice comes to one in the dark. (You as you always
were.) No one needs ever to say alone aloud. Yet and again. Imagine.
A way. A tone.

Along the river-run. Pebbles. Peppercorns. Nipples. Mean
the world to me. Literally. Paper feels potent to me. Like a water gun,
I imagine, does in a little kid's hands.

That is, one small figure leaves an ellipsis. Then the other,
as a matter of course, does not.

Take the not-blind people. I try to draw a straight line from
them to me. But it's impossible. Without a ruler, a rule means
nothing.

My friend the deaf boy tries to make checkers into chess. He
adores numbers, especially 137 because this is the angle at which one floret
of the sunflower grows into another, best suited for occupying space
over the growing time of the plant.

The body, he says, can generate excellent cathedral plans. In
the dark, the room expands randomly like a tumor, but hardly more
than an emphatic rumor of the brass doorknob, the one to a room that
is so tarnished only I know its brass underneath.

Can you see? My eyes are open. They are open and I can see
people, but they are like trees, walking. Like stumps shuffling or fall
leaves crimped into brown flour.

What's blind ecstasy like? A couple who clinks wine glasses
together until they break. Then drink. Drink. Drink.

Sometimes maybe I do get too drunk. Don't care. I'm not the least bit sorry for it. Don't care. I am a walleyed beast, but I'm not deaf. Listen. All rhyme holsters me into silence. Like an arrow waits patiently in a quiver.

And so I wait on a stair, stuck with infinity on a Tuesday afternoon, laughter boomeranging from another room. Laughter becoming a brittle hand, a candy cane snapped below its chin.

Leave the house? Who has the guts to do it? Even after 17 years, 17 years of doing it precisely the way it shouldn't have been done. (White wine in mother's oatmeal. A pocketful of Dutch licorice candies mistaken for change.)

I shouldn't lose out. I should add up my life, misplaced mirror by master mirror. The history of black on black.

Shouldn't I also be the first to tell you: I am Midnight's Mistress who shoes night's horses with thunder-colored shoes.

Look, I don't have a seeing-eye dog. I have a miniature pony. (They say he'll live longer; 40 years.) His name is Robby. The pony and I will grow old together, hating each other.

But, people try to be nice. Placing my hand on the deaf boy's hand, Mother says *Marry him*. Placing my hand on the Bible, Father says *Marry Him*. Opening the bedroom window letting in that fist of winter, Brother says *Marry the world*.

People try to be nice.

Let me put it this way: I've gotten younger knowing blindness better. Never mind callused fingertips. Endless circles. Never mind the golden mean has nothing to do with the golden rule.

I don't blame you. But I know you aren't enthusiastic about meeting me. You. A jar of rhinos. Or might as well be. Am I a briny fingerprint etched in isinglass? Blind or deaf? Salted or sugared? Separate but equal isn't pitiful.

Don't say of me that I didn't laugh in silent films; that I talked with a mouth full of blue and pink cotton candy; that I was a wise wound.

Say instead:

> She was a monocle in the army of glass.
> She agreed to take on the nth degree.
> And she won and was, at arm's length, undone
> By what she loved enough but did let go.

Pastoral

In the field the woman is
        alone. How long
                is her April, her sonnet?

A turned-up parenthesis
        hangs over her head,
                like an umbrella catching rain.

She is aware of
        a piece of string plumbed down
                from the sky

but does not let on to it.
        There is plenty to do.
                She whacks at a weed but hits

a black radish.
        The sun drops the full length
                of her body as lemons drop

from a table,
        one by one,
                rot.

Songs of Salience and Ambience

If the hymen is a hymn
if the hymen is a hymn

Singing
girls singe

Because boys melt away
like snow in May

As if there were
no such cold thing

Index of Lawn Bowling or Index of Teenage Intimacy

Chalking
Challenged
Changing During Play
Colliding
Damaged
Dead
Disallowed
Ditched, Non-Toucher
Ditched, Toucher
Inspection
Labels, Attached to
Lifting to Avoid Collision
Omitting to Play in Turn
Outside of Rink
Playing Another's
Premature Delivery
Rebounding, Non-Toucher
Rebounding, Toucher
Replayable
Testing on Green
Touchers
Wrong Bias, Penalty for

Trireme

I.

When people are alone, they often behave as if they were not; and when in
      company, they often behave as if they were alone.

Although it must be taken for granted that certain individuals behave differently
      when alone than when with others,

The conclusion seems inevitable that the human being as a social animal chiefly
      behaves as if it were almost always in a social situation.

At least for the scientific observer this seems a safe assumption to make; at most
      and more often than not,

It will minimize those errors that were made when the human being was
      assumed to be solitary:

A point of destination as well as a point of origin.

II.

It is no coincidence that you cross your fingers when you say "ready" in sign
      language.

III.

"I went for the wood last time," you say. And I look up from the black pot on
      the stove and, still smiling, say, "You went all the way to Paris."

Character in the Real World

There had been so many, so courageous in their particulars
and so foolhardy in their generalities, no offense
to any of them, the dalliances and the self-titled true loves,
the wiggy tenors and heroic sopranos, but none

of my fellow travelers fit the lifelong bill. And I know
I hadn't fit theirs either. It wasn't anybody's fault, though
it had been necessary, only natural, that those someones
along the way had to take their spankings because

of the unhappiness of both monogamy and celibacy. I
figured having a baby would be a good way to meet women
semi-unprepared, like the faithful walking of the dog
in the park. Perhaps take in a couple of weekend marriages

without the chronic habit and flawed contract. A baby
would give me the family, the little friend I'd always dreamed of.
(I didn't come here for the money.) Trouble was, finding
that certain lover who would have the little dumpling

and then abandon me, us. At first I thought I could
simply get an old friend to do the job, but of course
that was easier written than read, so I decided
to start my parentage in any case by getting a cat.

I don't know why I didn't go with a dog, probably
because I've always been under the impression
that dogs are men and cats are women and I don't like men
all that well, though I am one of them. Them. Those people.

You people who can't fit with you other people.

Stone Fruit

You're not supposed to think of the ballerina's
big toe being crushed inside her silk slipper.

Sure, the clitoris is amazing: it has no onus
but for pleasure. An exponential function.

The divine officer without peers. Soldiers trudging,
artillery pumping, buildings collapsing, boats

bumping ashore. But for the woman who has never had
an orgasm, it's an abstract atrocity. A plastic haw.

Orgasm this, orgasm that. She says:
The bananas are brown. The grapes are spoiled.

The produce was put into the wrong bag.
She says: Maybe I can fake being upset.

You get a bad plum, maybe it's an act of God.

Gentle Boys

We five pretty girls are
in the room don't lie or be

silent pray O cosmic lock
pop that one's orthodoxic

hirsute door open see boys
we are chocolate deserts

but inside you can float
like a bob on the water

of a puddle so what
if our mouths open against

you all good things are
difficult to make easy

be more like us you will not
fail or fall but step lightly

we are beautiful holes
that load and anchor

Fable

Once upon a time
there was a lonely fox; she was
lonelier than a wooden rowboat in a field.

She happened to come to a hill,
and fell in love with the first wolf she saw.
Already she loved its long lashes

and its freckled wrinkles,
but the eyes stopped her.
Apart from God nobody ever

found those eyes as beautiful
as did this childlike beast.
So at night the fox went up the hill,

stopped before the set of eyes,
and never moved from there anymore.
She had wanted a life of chasing butterflies,

but instead stood by one mustard iris.
When, at last, the wolf opened its mouth
it was not to kiss the fox

but to let the world crawl in.

II

How They Existed in the World

Two for a dollar
postcards started "Dear."

Two magnolia leaves
under a pile of rakes.

Two old rock
stars after asylum.

Two thousand suns
without shade.

Two afghans wrapped
around a coat tree.

Two foreign idioms
in a crowded train.

Two Oriental rugs moored
by a red thread.

Progress

There is
(a) seduction in the going toward and going away or
                        (b) dissatisfaction in progress.

You have the choice to
(a) mind yourself or
                        (b) mine everyone else.

It is only
(a) a lust in the mirror or
                        (b) the supposition of a bust.

There is
(a) a death which waits for us or
                        (b) one which does not.

That kisses
(a) kissed enough become stones or
                        (b) only break the seal.

You may
(a) not need this information now or
                        (b) want to go to bed.

What's left for you is
(a) the page of a book or
                        (b) the back of a heartthrob's head.

"When I don't know what you're thinking,
(a) I feel like I'm going blind or
                        (b) I am blind."

Top Story

When I learned of my love affair with you,
I thought good news! But it was
getting to be a routine: this guy died, that gal died.

It was getting to be like *who died today?*
But no, this time was different. It was
a perfect day for a portrait. What photographers call

the soft box: a gray day. I'd just been re-reading
part of my memoirs in the park: "Goodbye
sweet embouchure, I must leave you

though it splits all my reeds." Oh, how
weary I was getting of my bad and my good.
Must a cucumber be sliced to enter

my harem? And how could I ever
contemplate our future and get anything else
done? They say, you must not force sex

to do the work of love or love to do
the work of sex, but I'm not completely convinced.
I mean, something has got to work somewhere,

even if in reverse. And besides
I'd gotten married on the weekends all those years—
cooking bacon and pancakes in the kitchen

on Sundays—when I should have been
in front of the TV necking! And then I read
your letter again. The one where the man and the other

woman had trouble on page one
but patched it up by page seven—the bastards!
You wrote that the sea of fools had parted for us,

and lo and behold I had to agree seeing
there were Easter eggs in the sky. And you
continued: *Look, my dear, we're gonna be stars!*

But that's where I drew what little I had
left of the line. When we met up that night,
I said, "I cannot come everyday to woo,"

and stiffening, "just because I don't want you
to go doesn't mean I want you to come back."
"But please," you said, "set your pearl-handled

pistol on the nightstand. Life has to go on."
And I said, "Are you sure?" But that was pressing
too much. You had turned to watch the TV,

and I turned just in time to see the camera
panning back and out and the heroine tumbling
over, into the abyss, still lacing her shoes.

Two-Pack Solitaire

That hand of yours represents
An elegant route

Snowed-

Out
Where sleeves come from

Dummy

(I only want you
To love me & you)

Like a perfectly potholed surface

We are
Or a cup of wine

Crushed

Sometimes lovers lie
Together

Sometimes a lay is all
We're good for

Saturday Night

after a crime scene photograph

There was a banging on the wall again and frankly
I wasn't sure whether I was going to answer it
this time, like I had that one time with
the assistant curator of the Museum of Egyptology
and that other one time with the director. . . .
Ah, but the light was marvelous out that night.
The sun on Michigan Avenue had hung the purple sky
so that my lollipop glowed a casino orange.
And though I never could stand a city
where everyone called the pigeons *doves*, I had just
taken in a good movie where the main character said
to the other main character, after being beaten up,
it hurts to breathe, and the reply was,
the reply was, *of course it does*—and then, I had to
get the door because your suddenly-naked
little bottom was making all those shadows
on the wall, and I simply took what came
into view no matter I had no tripod,
no guts, no wind in the victim's gorgeous hair.

My One and Only Love No. 9

Let me say ahead of time I'm sorry, I knew
what I was doing. Three cigarettes out of four,
five business suits out of six, I knew what I was

doing. The cashmere coat laid beside the tequila
shot on the piano bench, the silly little contusion
before the brightly lit sin, I knew what I was

doing. Extra mindful of shaky ceiling fans and cracked
picture frames, burglar alarms and keyboards,
forgotten skewers and atomizers, I knew

what I was doing. Of so many engagement rings
caught in seat belts, of peanut butter in shag rugs,
of burnt out light switches and sperm-strewn bath towels,

I knew what I was doing. Liminal state by limit,
roller skate over rolling rocks, mailbox aside
breadbox, I knew what I was doing. One sprinkler

in the yard, one more prediction at the tale's end,
one less phone call and trash can, I knew
what I was doing. All along boardwalks and freckled

throats, all with plastic wreaths and lawnmowers,
in time for doorbells and dripping water faucets,
I knew what I was doing. Because with forgiveness

as with machines, with tapestries as with rows of
tombstones, with overstuffed loveseats as with last
lines, and because the soup of my apology kept getting

colder and the free admission at the backdoor stopped
feeling like a half-hearted confession, I cried,
"Partial! Platonic! But I was holding his bloody hand!"

Terms of Attraction (Greek Legend for Americans)

BLUE: Like a newly found bruise, one that recurs, not exactly all the time, more than sometimes, never fully. Slightly less than licit: a length of time that lasts a lifetime, your lifetime, hardly like anybody else's.

BRILLIANT: Sharp or dull, often liable, the speaking likeness of a pain or wound. The imitation of cranes, something that draws a new red line or illustrates the unwillingness to budge formally or fashionably.

ENIGMA: The game of games, something misunderstood, ill-understood, or not understandable, but engaged in nevertheless like mourning morning. A mistake made like a knot for someone else to undo.

GARDEN: A place for sinners in the holy city. A kiss swollen shut, a heavy door that crushes a left foot, a space in which to hide a ridiculous paranoia, a panic, or a pair of cold feet.

LOOP: The impossibility of guessing how many pebbles fill the washed-out grape jelly jar. Looking outside for a guarantee, a last-minute hook-up, a last stay against the forces of wish evaporation.

PASSPORT: To travel on a divan, lying down, watching the land, people, cities, and ruins passing by. Low energies wiped across large distances for the purpose of identification and, if necessary, intercourse.

RESTRAINT: Cross-hatched salt grass, mettle of nettles, metal against metal, how to open a strongbox, how to play with a thimble. A pressure put upon a single moment, a way of loving that moment too much or not ever enough.

TOMATO: Smaller than a watermelon, larger than an olive, the color of fresh blood: the mitochondria of the salad. Strong, carnal, the right red in tender. The tin can kind permissible in a pinch. In house wars, the object thrown or un-thrown or simply resting on the kitchen table waiting to be consumed at any cost.

UNCERTAINTY: A heavenly mana transformed into a mantra: "Zero is my hero."

VARIATION: A pattern of alternating currents especially the type zapped through a hand glazed with cloudy bath water. The vibration between chill and crunch, maintained by a lot of pleading. A fatal while.

WALK: A path of undetermined length and stride ending in a make-up, a fight, or a draw. Never neutral, always inviolable, always in the way of something else of equal importance, e.g. sitting, sipping tea, screwing, screaming.

YOGURT: The color of fair confidence, akin to free ice cream during a depression. A semi-solid food, soured but succulent, often enhanced unnecessarily with honey, fruit, or spices.

YOU: As in a dried starfish or a dying breath that becomes more beautiful with age. Looking into the beloved's eyes and seeing oneself, there in miniature, which done long enough results in a baby. Pre-procreation. That is, a pair of "gazing babies" for which a palliative nurse will never be rid of. Alternatively, grabbing grace for all it's worth; kicking a percentage back.

Second Honeymoon

He has built a safe harbor.
She has managed the honey.

Both have grown
into mature women.

The kitchen might be a bitch
and the bedroom a chore

but it's still best
to do laundry before lunch.

No matter. Here they are
eating their nest egg

for breakfast. Soon
they will make love like old

and a body will float ashore
with its pockets turned inside out.

Missteps in the Ballroom

i.
But the woman is not,
        as it happens, falling
                swiftly. She could
wink until her contact pops
        out, but that's no
                guarantee of landing
a date. Everybody
        wants a last snap
                from her true vine.

{To the guidebooks!}

But why contemplate marriage,
        the man thinks,
                on account of a well-
used button?

        ii.
        In modern dictionaries
                the radical for "heart"
appears in two
        versions. One simplified
                and the other shown
here: {Hello, My name
        is ——————— }.
                It's true, the man says.
I only have one testicle.
        Logic chopped the other
                off. People like me try
to be machines, or is it
        machines that try
                to be like people?

{Someday we'll know.}

iii.

The absent ball is
        simply the a
                of atypical. Nothing
more. Getting it
        snipped was like
                having my blood
pressure taken: a semi-
        pleasurable, short-
                lived strangulation.
What they don't tell
        you: a missing ball
                makes the flesh

iv.

fall and the heart
        grow legs. Sweat
                beads turn into real
beads; real beads gather
        not like a bunch of
                white grapes in a crystal
bowl, but like the hand-
        written prayers of orphans
                to their nonexistent
mothers. What isn't
        more beautiful
                with a bit of blood on it?

v.

The sun isn't a sign
        but a fiery button.
                Use your thumb to cover
the sun and you'll see
        what I mean. In other
                words: if the weather is nice,
we'll probably go out.
        Why do we, after all,
                sometimes laugh when children
cry? We get hold of
        one, and miss the other.
                Imperfect is actually perfect.

                {Let's cut the bullshit.}

      vi.

A paper cut is perfect.
        An accident with a
                flame-thrower is perfect. Death,
a movie star in her bath,
        is perfect. We're all
                perfectly cut by the same knife.
So when the woman and the man
        finally break up, it is like
                a dime severed in half, very
unlike two
        spinning
                nickels.

Queen of Tarts

She doesn't need to be a star
or have a mob of one surround her.

She just wants to know should she
be rich or should she be poor?

How the queen wants it all to mean
something more when she talks

her way in the front door. A broken
nose for a corsage, a coral snake

for a sash, two corkscrews for eyes.
When the armies of penitence come

to feel up her blouse, Lady
Liberty lets go her blue ditty:

"He was the jungle and the ballroom
and he might have been the Devil

but he had better lines than God.
He wrote: the war goes on, friends die,

good weather . . . my first mistress
(the most desirable woman in Paris)

fucked me for the laughter not the heroics."

Blue-Sky Law

Oh it's hard, isn't it—bunion hard, to move on
because he is so far away. How do you know
that it's only lust? Not that you can't use

the same trope again and again. You don't
want stasis. You want him. If he's wrong
for you, you'll probably have to drink

the dirty bath bilge. If he's right for you,
you'll have to burn up the entire paper
shrine of your little flesh-eating heart. Fair

day. Both of you know the Copernican principle
holds that there's nothing special about your
place in the universe. And yet, you two might be

alone. So what if he lets the water for tea boil
away, or if he can never remember to reach over
and unlock the car door. Indeed, why shouldn't

you care about him? In a moment of weakness,
it's fine to be holding somebody else there
in the foyer, as long as you keep eyeing his

photo on the mantel. Who said people who love
each other should be able to get along? First
it's yes, then it's maybe. A love story is not a boy

and a girl running through tall grass, but rather
two bodies meeting the moment an open
window lets the rain in, right before the blankets

get damp. When you want to be moved,
you don't buzz around the house crowing,
I'm feeling so emotional! No. You put on

a little music, lay on the davenport balled-up
in bedspread and sleep it off. Why insist on
dropping a ton of bowling balls on each other's toes

when we all know one does the job well enough?
Because the cowardly love we have of freedom
can't refuse cruelty. He often asks: *But really*—

how do you *feel?* And you think of that fluke
phone call that arrived seemingly out of nowhere
and those words you once wrote him, *kissed briefly*

and just because. Yes. You do have to remember that
even in Australia there are bad days. That even
with a paucity of orchestral knowledge you may

twitter again in the high winds, and how putting
your wet finger in the air is only to get a sense
of direction, not a direction itself. But

what have you been doing all day long? Focus
and refocus. Getting too late now for more
discussion. You really must go. Try to understand.

There's Chinese food burning on the stove
at home, and you have to get the bedroom
painted. You promised him a sky-blue.

A Play

The trellis is shaking with guards
as the curtain opens:

Despite the lost battle, the queen accepts
the knight without question.

He lifts up the saliva-blue sheet, as if
unwrapping gauze.

He watches her legs rub together.
"Take these butter knives," she says.

He drops his forget-me-not cloak
over the bed and prunes his beard.

She can't believe it's that hard
to fool disappointment.

They crush the bedstraw mattress
and she opens her mouth

plump with jewelweed and marriage.

Modern American Scenes for Student Actors

I. Man, Woman, Taxi Driver

The man's love is a tiresome halftime. This is nothing new for the man who's nicknamed The Incredible Shrinking Lover by his wife. He freely admits he's blind, figuratively of course. "Let's neck," the woman says. { } "See, it's impossible for him to do it eyes open." On the weekends, the woman goes to the airport to kiss her imaginary boyfriends goodbye. But there are too many of them. Thus, the short answer to the love of the man and the woman is "I do." And the long answer is "I should have married David Rabinowitz."

(Note: The man's ability to love is inversely related to the size of his ego which is inversely related to his penis size. This does not mean his love and his penis are the same size.)

II. Peter, Sarah, Stranger 1, Stranger 2, Police Officer, Coroner

This is on a busy street. Sarah loses her husband, Peter, to strangers. Not to strangers exactly, but to the kindness of strangers. The strangers (there are two of them, a couple you could say even though they aren't holding hands) notice that a fellow citizen has left his car headlights on. They go over to check the door. Damn thing is locked. While they are checking the door, they leave the driver's side door of their own car wide open. Peter, Sarah's husband in case you're confused, is riding his bicycle looking up at the sky and doesn't see the wide-open door. This is the accident happening. The front bicycle tire, brand new, smacks the inside of the car door and Peter the Husband goes not-flying over the top of the door and plops down on the pavement headfirst. Trouble is, he has been writing one of the most beautiful poems ever written in the history of poem writing, that very morning, and the final line is coming to him just as he hits the car door.

(Note: The strangers interpret Peter's death as a suicide.)

III. Between 1 and 127 Actors

If you were in charge of reforming society after some cataclysmic event, what would you do first?

    a) Build better schools.
    b) Print multicolored money.
    c) Create a new language.
    d) Shit your pants.

(Note: Base your answer on a two-thirds majority vote.)

IV. Lecturer, Students, Stuffed Animal, Chorus

The lecturer is a person who must talk for an hour. The student is a person who must listen for the bell. The lecturer does not ring the bell; the student does not ring the bell either. After much discussion, in fact, nobody in the room knows who the bellringer is. But no one is leaving until the bell rings.

The lecturer draws a circle on the chalkboard, roughly the circumference of a large pizza. The students surmise that the lecturer is in deep contemplation, still facing the chalkboard, back to the class. But all the lecturer thinks about, as it were, is a childhood stuffed animal named Lucy.

"And then the mouth, she . . . she—" one of the students begins to say, but is cut off by the lecturer who lets out a brief, if explosive, high-pitched scream.

Sounds like a dog's yelp, thinks Rachel.

Like a pimple popping, writes Scott in his notebook.

Like what am I doing here, mumbles Charlie.

The lecturer turns back around and faces the class. He whispers: "What was that?"

Someone in the back accidentally knocks a full paper cup of coffee on the floor. A few students clamor *shit*, and someone hurries out of the room for the women's bathroom where there are neither paper towels nor toilet tissue, just a hand-dryer which no one ever uses. The student looks at the hand-dryer for a few long seconds and then she rushes out of the bathroom again, remembering some napkins in the glove box of her car parked illegally in staff lot B.

The coffee, meanwhile, has been wiped up by another student with a ratty gym towel taken from his duffel bag.

The lecturer never forgets what he was about to say, and the students never find it odd that the bell never rings.

(Note: As a member of the chorus, your task is to create the lecture that has yet to and will not occur.)

Matinee

The house is too cold;
he's left all the goddamn windows open again.

And what if it rains, the winds and wet linens—
you'll need a whiskey.

Lie down a spell,
there, in the sheltered garden next to Schubert.

You want to ask him why you're still together,
when all could be divided.

Might you undo his yellow
raincoat and grab the hair from his shuffling skin—

You can,
but you don't have to. At the end of the day,

let his shadows do the work. He will fall to you
as an apron full of seeds.

Aerialist

He's still as tall as ever,
the love of your life,

not quite bearable up there.
Impossible to ignore

like a borrow pit
already fallen into,

or a scratch in the skin:
crimson then gold,

haphazard then designed.
His first act was

matter-of-fact;
the second crackled

like alcohol over ice;
and now the penultimate:

all eyes on the ceiling,
the equator between

you two, a cathedral
of air and nerve.

Love (IV)

This is the floating
mine

or
"internal machine"

the deceiving fish
apparent

This is the proving
device

for powder burns
for the sound

the ratchet-wheel makes
against the spring

This is the pistol-shaped
buoy

wrought-up
of curry, coal, and ice

III

Nocturne

If time is the sky,
Then moments are understandable

Autumns, the leaves split
Seconds, and sorrow is
Undressing the neighbor boy

In a single breath.
If such gusty emotion is

The landscape, words make
Only the mountains, and the valleys
Are just gorgeous inversions.

And if the head sounds
Like that, each drop of rain

An amorous dialogue,
Then leave tonight,
Between the wave and the lantern,

Every particle
Rowing.

The Teller Is the Only Survivor of the Fairy Tale Ending

On the eve of never departing at least there are no bags
to pack or last breaths to send away
with the last storybook lover. How lyrical it is

to be off to nowhere. No sore heart
nor new fist, no new heart nor sore fist,
no one soaring or sore at all.

But if I hear a pair of voices
coming between noises coming
from the guest room, it must be bedtime again:

I chase a couple one way across the ditch,
over a hill, through the neighbor's orchard and field.
I chase them back toward home,

corner the two against a fence.
Then after a lot of praying, I pull the keys
from the dead man's pocket while cupping her

breath in my hands. It sounds like a foolish thing
to do: to stop a couple of heartthrobs,
between If and Then.

But telling is a terrifying
beauty, who gives and gives and gives out
prematurely. All the sadness in life

lies in the present moment.
It's not that the characters truly remember being
born, but that's The Story.

I, The Teller, promise them the future
lasts a long time. And then I head into the unending
rain with a borrowed umbrella,

one I have no intention of ever giving back.

Come Back My Daughter from the Green Fjords

To him who marries and marries and marries—
gael, giddy, gall—bear it out! With borrowed resolve,
I sent my twinkling troops back into the cemetery.
This time, however, the man with the violin case wasn't talking.
I was embarrassed that all my guests had brought such charming gifts
and I'd forgotten the sugar at the store. Had I time to dig out
a new sugar lane to the neighbor's before the grand event?
No. I'd have to compromise once more. Scraped the icing
off the hard tack and onto the angel food cake and announced
"finger food," as if I were a pig who knows he's dinner.
Ten beatings later, maybe more, my servants screamed
bloody murder! It was about time. I didn't know how long
any of us were going to keep this up. A frail layer of ice
maintains itself only so long before completely cracking
under the weight of heavy breath. People were getting restless,
so I made a peace offering: "A round of tears for everybody,
on me!" But nobody drinks anymore. The head chef was
especially perplexed at the state of events, since he'd gotten up
extra early that morning. I know, because it was slightly after
I noticed that my Anna Livia had run away. And there again was
the cake to remind me of the great escape from the bedroom
ledge. The work of thieves posing as firefighters. My slit
satchel fully emptied of seeds. I threw open all the windows
and screamed to the trees, Nest or fly! Nest or fly!

A Lover's Education

I am trying to learn how to cook. In perfection class,
they told me I added a little too much sugar.
That I blanched one too many mensches. Overly self-

conscious: tisk-task. Sweethearts all look good
from a distance. But what makes them turn saccharine?

The basic scenario involves being tied up in old
raven's lace, I imagine. What is bored ecstasy like?
Contretemps. The feeling you are supposed to feel

while attending a funeral but can't, because
you don't have any feelings for the dead in question.

Oh hell. I can fake an epiphany. Poison
a sacred wafer. Bake big, easy bread pudding.
What buys the bed while wits borrow the bedclothes:

good intentions. Both love and sex. Icebergs
in paradise. Since all is war that ends war,

and one world burrows in on another—forgetting
is out. And Dutch courage is in. I've learned
there are no artificial tears, only mispronunciations

of the word. Here's the smiling congé: I admit
I've served my children frozen peas. Negatively

caloric foods. Yes. Peas sound like glass tears
when they hit the plate, one by one. But
all of them falling at once, sounds like applause.

Double Portrait

The Man With Two Shadows had sixty-four lovers,

not an outrageous number
as compared to the Invisible Man's Daughter.

When they met, he was circling the loaves of bread
and she was standing in the aisle.

She asked if he was a race car driver.
She asked if he liked Saturdays or Sundays best.

He said she looked like an ice cream princess.
He said he could see her legs, they looked like curtains

and that her face was cream with whole strawberries.
Despite their flaws, they got hitched. As it turns out

The Man With Two Shadows liked Sundays best
and the Invisible Man's Daughter liked Saturdays,

so they married on a Monday and never looked back,
for their marriage was perfect on weekdays.

He distrusted sunbeams, poetry, the precious;
precisely those binds of artifice to which she was devoted.

As she expressed it, "He wants to pinch my bottom.
I want to preserve my illusions."

She tells him he has no grace in a gallery.
He turns to touch her, as if to ask a question about this or that,

and she is still not there.

Traveler

What you need is an allegory. What you get is a flight tracker. A 747 darned
with popes into the sky. You want to believe the heavens can contain every
possible blue, every deaf ending, every brilliant asshole that should go down—
down to the weakest sucking noise a lover makes quaffing before orgasm.

A girl dreams and dreams of growing a perfect tit. A businessman next to her
wants to trim her hair while she sleeps. His high hopes break off, piece by
piece. The plane lumbers through rough haze, the color of her eyes.
And the music in his ears begins to see clearly the terror of his prayers.

The hours pile up. The man doesn't know whether or not to use the emergency
exit to get to heaven. In her sleep, the girl has sold him her body for nothing. He
sits there very still, entranced by her ugly ear—hammer and drum—which is
bleeding like a small bird.

Dear Birds

Much is made of the size of your heart.
Or the way some of you pull an earthworm
to death. Compare for example, this portrait
of my husband, the artist, three cocktails in:

Fish in the morning, fellatio in the afternoon,
philosophizing after dinner. Sucking on
a hazelnut in haze and hard rain, he pulls off
it all: pain, politeness, and unemployment.

I admit, it does please me to think of him
mourning my death. Tissue by tissue, he'll paint
the orange groves and narrow bridle paths.
He'll arrange colors like music that coats the ear.

So is heartache really a mistake? The question is
realer than any answer can be: One comes upon
the hills and then the pills. But not everyone,
my little sugar skulls, can eat their mistakes.

Every Force Deserves a Form

Why are young widows mourning so attractive?

A) They almost always wear black, diaphanous underthings.
A) They have pretty luminous noses and eyes like burnished beads.
A) They like to stay up late.
A) They don't give a damn about joining the choir.
A) The world is most shot through with collateral beauty.

Reverence

I said, "I married
my childhood sweetheart, this morning,
along with seven other ex-lovers."
The priest said, "Congratulations. It was inevitable."

"Truth is," I said,
"I loved them all until I left them.
That was inevitable . . .
Why'd you become a priest?"

"You have two eyes, my son.
Have you seen the rectory's nuns?"
"Why, yes, kind of . . .
can't see much behind their habits," I said.

"Most secrets go unnoticed," he said and waited.
"I admire statements I can't prove," I said and waited.
He said, "Try this one: tenuous marriages
allow for great victories of the heart."

"Then you truly have seen what's behind
the nun's costume . . . ?" I said.
"There's a $100 chance of rain today," he said.
"But don't spend it all . . ."

And I saw his smile decline.
"My son, you must become like
a naked nun standing before the mirror. You
must sing in a private choir."

Reluctant Prophet

And for example, I,
Jonah, am large
in my way. Little

by little, tooth
by tooth, the body swells;
bits fit in, the sound of

herringbone teeth;
the pieces unfold, neat
and distinct, the end

circuit leaves a handful
of shit. This—the whale's
inky body, my body

of work—a shadow
when two things touch.
We cut into the sea.

The sky an echo of
ice. The beast cuts into
me. My voice: a toy

crow, a ripple, a thigh,
the whole fleshy
fever, sextan.

Gentle Reader

You might like some of the poems at once, but you mustn't be surprised if your taste differs from the rest of the class. If you like the sea, there is a poem on p. 49 to start on; if you enjoy reading about "battles long ago" (even though you think wars today are unnecessary, silly, and violent), go to p. 22, or see the stirring ballad of "Weathercock and Firefly," p. 31. If you like poems about nature, you might try "Seaman's Breath"; or, if you prefer humorous poetry, you might start with "The Devil and the Marmoset." And then, there's everyone's greatest joy and incense: "Love Poems," which you will find, like the French, everywhere and nowhere at once, but especially on p. 8 with "A Little Morning After Poem."

After a time you'll realize that you can have good poems about every subject under the sun, and you don't have to be fond of the subject or the sun in order to like the poem. For example, you may have a horror of cats and yet enjoy "Cat's Beef Brisket"; you may think it lunacy to believe in fairies and mermaids, and yet take delight in the poem titled "On p. 32." You may think that men are ugly but discover a poem about them that is handsome.

So. If you don't like a poem at first, it doesn't necessarily mean it is a bad poem or that the poet and the muse haven't done their jobs. Not every good poem need move you, even if it has caused its owner perfect pain and sufficient sadness. A little this about that: while Theseus or Shakespeare may have been having a little joke in that last scene of A Midsummer Night's Dream, the lunatic, the lover, and the poet can't be happy all the time and can't be sad all the time. Still, it is important to recall that all true artists must cultivate pain: remember mother.

I do not countenance giving advice to strangers; however, before you begin the poems you should make a resolution never to pretend to like a poem you really find dull. Unless you are quite honest in your likes and dislikes you will end up hating poems altogether, and that would be a predicament. O.

On Raisins

They are much misunderstood.

Like that old writer's truism:
"Write what you know"—well,

you don't know very much.
So you write about raisins.

Faithless little fuck-ups,
plucked, dried, smashed in a box.

That feeling of being in the world,
but not of the world. So what

if berries fall from the hand
as only berries do.

Poem

The peephole of my door is aligned with your keyhole—
how can that still be! With one hand
I open the door a little. But the trembling
in the other makes me overly critical. Two thousand

lamps illuminate this room, but I can't cast
a lucid shadow on your door. My mind says,
please step into the hallway and wait your turn
on so-and-so's side of the velvet rope.

See, I don't have to list off the world's capitals,
or play my clarinet, or write about a sparrow's death
to get at your little heart. And I have guts—
why just this morning I blasted a friend

for praising fiction over poems and for chagrinning
the ordinary sun. Once you and I looked at
the sky, then we looked at the earth
through the window, but now we look at the window—

what does that mean? Let me elaborate:
Don't let those Parisian bedbugs bite,
unless of course one is named Othello and he plays
his lullaby on the oboe. Yes,

we have many faces. Yours was prettier than mine.
But we weren't pretty. I mean, our loveliness
couldn't afford to stay at home while the world waited
alone. I might not be able to throttle you

to death with my heart straps, but I can stab you
with your own bobby pin. Don't make me
talk when I want to go to bed, or go to bed
when I want to kiss. My eyes may be flickering,

my head may be warped, but it is clear as rain
that you still eat onion sandwiches in the Victory Garden.
You drive your convertible through the hills,
your hat on tighter than before, your teeth reflecting the sun—

you wear blues—but they don't match!
There's a coffee stain on your picture
and I want to clean it, as soon as I can figure out how
to get to myself without opening your door.

Yours and Some of Mine

To be wanted before you're wanted, painting
flesh in a badly lit room. To run away,
figure slapped over ground,

quickly and clumsily, then perfectly
smoothed in, as if by small rhapsodic blows
to the sternum. To take those short

precluded trips to the minimal
hotel in town, to the lobby, to that chair
from which I, Infinite Reader, watch

a man's hand slightly touch the blue-
belted hip of his lover. I heard you
clear your throat periodically. The hours

I was obliged to watch, with lips pulled away,
a supernumerary copy of your figure
reappearing as ground, vanishing

into what was never really there.

Old Celery

At the corner greengrocer
I'd passed you many times before,
always under the bright lights,
water beading up on your tough skin.

I picked up a tomato,
a pair of kohlrabi,
a handful of coriander;
I had money this time.

As I counted my change,
a penny dropped down under your stand.
On the way up, you,
old celery, caught my eye.

You'd been moved to a darker corner
of the produce. I now felt
guilt; I had missed
you in your prime.

I set down the other vegetables,
took you, limp and barely
green, and left a hollow yellow
in the bed of shaved ice.

When I held you up
to get a fair look, there was
not a silence in the world
like the silence between us.

Like so many things I've not wanted
to see until they persisted
in seeing me, I took you
as if now I had a choice.

Against Elegy

Still on this side of time—
        hands interlocked,
                no prayer—try

to hang on
        like the hinge of
                a sign that flashes

Applause!
        Applause!
                Applause!

Because if the present,
        the flawless sound
                of a treadle sewing

machine, closes up
        nicely enough, the scar
                leaving the skin—

You will run a trail
        to leave a trail.
                No meter for grief.

Good Mouth

You go so still.
You believe in miracles
Only an orphan remembers.

You know as well
As I do, this necklace of sleep
Is imitation.

From many dining room habits,
One rule: don't fight me
While I slurp hot soup.

But baby me like
Bottom. Occupy me.
Then rest like a pheasant

Shot out of season,
Or a flute bubbling
To the bed of a lake.

Don't believe the news
Is always serious when the centerpiece is
A box of tissues.

You're Either Harriet or Harry

The piano burning in the foreground blows
you away, as it were or you'd like it to. The last

in a series of drinks and a conversion to sidecars.
You weren't brave, but you gave pleasure. The trouble

with smashing academic pigeon-holes is that
the hole does lend itself to do certain things.

There's knowledge in the slots like there's knowledge
in sonnets. What anyone struggles against, that

saws are dangerous and then insanely still. Saws
sound nothing like sleep. This is written in marble

in gold letters: Here a girl lived and played and
died. And I'm not sure how many characters

her life took. But I know she can always use another
friend. I watch the dead like I watch commuters

inhabit their shadows along the buildings
at sunset. My favorite promised people. They

carry secret papers home, then easily sleep.
When they rise, they do what they do when

they fall. They don't wait for the curtain call.

Self Portrait with Still Life

And travel to the farthest ends,
        leave Hickory Star,
                Shady Valley, and Kepler.
There is an opening
        at the end of a string,
                a friendship
for solitude. Give out
        your name as a world
                capital, a complication,
a promise to be continued.
        Find the difference
                of opinion that marks
a point of interest,
        a mistake avoided
                then gone back for.
Amass an interest
        in anticipation,
                an anticipation of drawing
water in war. Take the hand
        waving, the head
                shaking, the audience
as evidence, as dust
        reveals sunlight between columns.
                Because in everything
wanted and not had,
        still the promise
                of a password
overheard;
        the possibility
                of exchanging
silences
        over the vegetables and fruits
                ripening.

Notes

The title of this book comes from a caption underneath a photograph of a group of people waiting for a stoplight to change in *Nonverbal Communication: Notes on the Visual Perception of Human Relations* (University of California Press 1956), a collaboration between the psychiatrist Jurgen Ruesch and the poet Weldon Kees; the latter is believed to have run away to Mexico or committed suicide by jumping off the Golden Gate Bridge.

The epigraph is adapted from Richard Zenith's translation of Fernando Pessoa's poem "Ah! They want a light that's better than the sun's," attributed to Pessoa's heteronym Alberto Caeiro (*Fernando Pessoa & Co.*, Grove Press 1998).

"The Mountain" is a loose piece of ekphrasis from the Balthus painting of the same title.

The poems "You Are Not a Statue" and "Matinee" were originally written in English, translated into Danish by Eva Green, and then retranslated into English.

"Before Losing Yourself Completely to Love" is for Cami.

"The Invisible Man's Daughter" borrows its first line from Charles Simic's poem "The Return of the Invisible Man" (*Jackstraws*, Harcourt 1999).

"Prose Sonnet" adapts a line from a short story by the philosopher Roger Scruton. This poem is for Ewa.

The beginning of "Blind Girl's Litany" adapts the first few lines of Beckett's novella *Company*. The line "I can see people, but they are like trees, walking" is from Mark 8:24. The rest of the poem was composed in a deprivation tank in Newton, Massachusetts.

"Songs of Salience and Ambience" adapts two lines from George Herbert's "The Flower."

"Trireme" was originally attributed to the poet's female alter ego, and section I adapts some phrases from *Nonverbal Communication*.

"Fable" uses as a model Jaroslav Seifert's poem of the same title. This poem is for M.

The movie alluded to in "Saturday Night" is Hal Hartley's *Henry Fool*, about an itinerant poet who falls in love with Parker Posey.

"Terms of Attraction (Greek Legend for Americans)" was prompted by the paintings of Kim Krause and appeared in his catalogue "Greek Variations."

"Blue-Sky Law" is a term first used by Justice McKenna of the U.S. Supreme Court in 1917 regarding state securities regulations. McKenna wrote: "The name that is given to the law indicates the evil at which it is aimed, that is, to use the language of a cited case, 'speculative schemes which have no more basis than so many feet of blue sky.' "

"Love (IV)" is in homage to George Herbert.

"The Teller Is the Only Survivor of the Fairy Tale Ending" takes its first line from a Pessoa poem, "On the eve of never departing" (translated by Richard Zenith).

"Come Back My Daughter from the Green Fjords" borrows Anna Livia from Joyce.

"Every Force Deserves a Form" is a modification of the title of Guy Davenport's book of essays *Every Force Evolves a Form* (North Point Press 1990). The poem's first line is a modification of an epigram in Georg Christoph Lichtenberg's *The Waste Books* (translated by R.J. Hollingdale, New York Review of Books 2000).

"Gentle Reader" borrows language from Kenneth Muir's introduction to *Four Winds, A Poetry Anthology* (A. & C. Black, Ltd. n.d.).

"On Raisins" is for Ndugu.

For more about the poems, see *The B-Sides* at www.markyakich.com

Acknowledgments

Grateful acknowledgment is made to the editors and readers of the following publications in which some of these poems first appeared: *580 Split, American Letters & Commentary, American Literary Review, Another Chicago Magazine, Arts & Letters, The Café Review, Center, The Cortland Review, Crazyhorse, Cross-Connect, Denver Quarterly, Fence, Gumball, Hayden's Ferry Review, In Posse Review, Indiana Review, La Petite Zine, Mid-American Review, New Delta Review, Octopus Magazine, Passages North, Pif Magazine, Pleiades, River City, The Southeast Review, Spinning Jenny,* and *Spork.*

Thank you to Mary Leader for discerning the rabbi tying his shoes.

Thank you to Ray Buffalo (paint, scotch, gruyère), Andrei Codrescu, Annie Goldman, David Higginbotham, James Kimbrell, Cindy King, Ann Lauterbach, Shara McCallum, Scott McWaters (unbridled F.G.), Kim Magowan (order and reorder), Tom Russell, Sarah Schumann (beans), Andy Spear (B.R.), Stephanie Stavropoulos (support and grace), Steve Stewart, Ray Thibodeaux, Elizabeth Triplett, G.C. Waldrep, and Robert Weinstock. Thank you to James Galvin, Paul Slovak (Penguin), and the National Poetry Series.

Thank you to the writing programs at Louisiana State University, University of Memphis, and Florida State University.